FELL WALKER'S EQUIPMENT GUIDE

by

Malcolm Bostock

DALESMAN

DALESMAN PUBLISHING COMPANY LTD.
CLAPHAM, via Lancaster, LA2 8EB

First published 1992

© Malcolm Bostock, 1992

ISBN: 1 85568 045 9

Cover photograph courtesy Vango (Scotland)

Products highlighted in this guide are representative of a wide range of equipment manufactured to the same high standard of quality and performance. Omission of any manufacturer's product does not imply that it is not suitable. This is a guide and not a catalogue, and is intended to help customers recognise suitable products that match the standard typified by the examples discussed in a general rather than specific way.

Typeset by Lands Services, East Molesey, Surrey.
Printed by Hubbards Ltd, Dronfield.

Introduction

Selecting the right equipment
In recent years, the application of technology to equipment design, manufacture and materials composition has produced a range of products with the high standard of quality and performance demanded of it when used in the type of variable climatic conditions experienced in year-round mountain environments.

This information is designed to help you identify the type of equipment necessary for such environments in addition to matching it to your own particular needs, thus eliminating problems and dangers caused by unsuitable equipment.

What about the cost?
Initial outlay for good quality equipment is high, but long term, is a good investment. Although enjoyment and success can be gained from using cheaper, less well-made equipment, this often proves to be false economy and leaves safety and success to chance, particularly in winter and prolonged bad weather. With this equipment, you get what you pay for!

Equipment and experience!
Good quality equipment will help you cope with most year-round conditions. Meeting challenges successfully depends on experience as well as equipment. Survival only becomes a serious concern for those who go beyond the limitations of their experience and equipment. Knowing these limitations will allow you to enjoy the freedom of the hills year-round without being preoccupied with survival! Having the best equipment is no substitute for lack of experience!

1   The Clothing System

A variable climate means a variable clothing system to cope with
it. Bad weather is greatly amplified in mountains and exposed
places as well as being unpredictable. At any time of year protection from the elements is vital in these conditions. When
questioning the need to buy an expensive outdoor clothing system
consider the versatility needed to cope with the problem of
maintaining warmth in severe conditions in winter, staying dry in
prolonged damp weather at any time of year while at the same
time providing adequate ventilation during periods of high activity
in addition to complete protection against the elements. You begin
to appreciate the importance of specialised clothing designed to
meet these requirements, the development of which is reflected in
the cost.

In a cold and wet climate the aim is to feel comfortable by
staying warm and dry at all times. If you become cold and damp
your trip becomes nothing more than an endurance test. In winter,
clothing should provide insulation against the cold by trapping
warm air in layers and fibres, maintained by a protective layer of
shell clothing which is impervious to wind and rain.

Practicality is more important than appearance and style
although most top of the range clothing systems now incorporate
both. Prime considerations are: keeping warm (on occasions in
summer as well as in winter) and keeping dry (a consideration all
year round).

Keeping warm: body layers

Base layer clothing
The main purpose of base layer garments these days is to help
maintain body temperature by conducting (wicking) moisture
produced by perspiration along the fibres away from the body
during high activity. It then evaporates or is absorbed by the next
layer, leaving the skin dry. This greatly reduces the cold clammy
chilling effect caused by damp inner clothing once activity ceases
and body temperature drops. To enable the fibres to function
effectively it is essential that garments fit closely and stretch
considerably. The traditional thermal layer is only one aspect of

the clothing system and is worn immediately over the base layer. For less active pursuits or more severe winter conditions, slightly heavier-weight garments having a brushed backing or wool facing provide extra warmth.

Fabrics
The majority of base layer garments are made from synthetic fibres such as polypropylene (polypro) polyester (capilene and polartec) chlorofibre (rhovyl/modal) and polyamide (tactel). These fibres absorb little or no moisture and dry rapidly. Garments are usually graded and fall into three main categories these being lightweight, midweight and expedition weight. Wicking is produced when body heat pushes moisture away from the skin along the fibres to the outside of the garment. Alternatively some fibres are designed to disperse moisture to less effected areas of the garment where it can evaporate more quickly.

Natural alternatives to synthetics are silk and wool. Rather than wicking moisture, natural fabrics absorb moisture into the fibres leaving the surface next to the skin relatively dry. They work well until they become saturated thus losing ability to insulate. Silk is extremely comfortable next to the skin, feels warm when damp, can be worn year round and does not retain body odour. Garments include long or short sleeve tops with crew or high zip necks, matching legwear, inner gloves, socks and headwear.

Midwear

Fleece garments
Both first layer and midwear clothing should not only provide warmth during periods of inactivity in cold weather, but more essentially during prolonged activity in cold damp conditions particularly during heavy rain. This is when inner clothing is more likely to become damp either through sweat, excess condensation from shell garments or wind-driven rain finding its way into even the most well designed waterproof jackets.

In these conditions fleece comes into its own. Having a low water absorbancy factor, it is able to dry rapidly. This light, highly durable fabric offers warmth and comfort even when damp.

Fleece garments are produced from several weights and thicknesses of material, resulting in a wide range of garments in a variety of colourful styles offering a versatile and practical clothing system, doing away with the need for several layers of traditional clothing and providing a better warmth-to-weight alternative.

Single faced fleece

Shirts and pullovers made from very soft lightweight single faced fleece are suitable as both first layer and midlayer clothing in most conditions. In colder climates, they provide effective insulation when worn over a thermal base layer and topped with a wind-proof jacket. Having a high degree of stretch also makes them very comfortable to wear and ideal for pursuits requiring a high level of body movement.

Fleece garments. An important feature found on most such garments, particularly jackets, is the fully closeable high-neck fold-down collar (centre and right) designed to keep out wind and maintain warmth.

Double faced fleece

In colder more severe conditions, thicker medium weight double faced fleece garments are necessary to maintain insulation. Both sweaters and jackets are made from medium weight fabric and constitute the majority of fleece garments available at present.

The problem with fleece has always been its lack of wind resistance. To counter this, the addition of lightweight microfibre or pertex shells and linings to the fabric extend the versatility of fleece jackets, making them windproof and showerproof. At present, the ultimate in fleece jackets are those which incorporate a Gore-Tex 'windstopper' breathable lining. A thicker, heavier version of the double faced fleece is used on some jackets to produce a much warmer midwear garment.

Although recommended as mainly midwear garments, most fleece jackets can be worn year-round as outer garments in all but the most severe conditions. In prolonged wet weather, all fleece clothing including shell lined jackets, need the added protection of a separate waterproof/windproof shell garment.

Fleece jackets are also used by several manufacturers as part of their all-weather combination clothing systems which combine a fleece inner jacket with a breathable nylon shell outer, offering year round weather protection.

Features
Jacket designs include the half zip over-the-head smock styles and full zip standard styles. All have fully closeable high neck fold down collars which keep warmth in and snow and spindrift out. A press stud flap over the half zip or backing material behind full length zips is an advantage in cold winds. Most designs feature two zipped front pockets, while some include a zipped chest pocket. Close fitting cuffs and hem provide optimum warmth and those finished in Lycra dry out rapidly and feel very comfortable.

A generous cut under the arms will allow unrestricted arm movement without causing the jacket to ride up the back during climbing activity. Various styles incorporate different features, however the majority of fleece garments are made to a very high standard of quality and the main differences are between styles and designs rather than performance.

Fibrepile
Having similar characteristics to fleece, fibrepile has a thick fluffy polyester pile woven into a backing fabric. The thick pile provides good insulation, trapping warm air in the fur giving a good thermal layer. Due to the open weave, fibrepile is not windproof and needs the protection of a microfibre or pertex face fabric, or a separate waterproof shell garment in wet climates. Pile, is not as stretchy as fleece and becomes heavy when wet.

Fibrepile garments can be very warm particularly when worn directly over base layer clothing providing an excellent thermal layer in cold climates. A complete range of very lightweight windproof (pertex faced) pile clothing is now available which if used under proper conditions, cuts out several layers of traditional clothing. Latest styles are extremely well designed with consideration for ventilation, access to pockets and comfort.

Outer layer: Jackets

Jackets
Although layers of fleece or fibre pile together with a shell jacket provide an ideal year round clothing system, alternative outer jackets suitable for winter and cold conditions at other times of year are outlined here. Any item of outer clothing, particularly jackets if used as outer garments in winter should be warm and windproof, easily ventilated, at least showerproof with ability to dry quickly and hard wearing.

Design should be practical with well positioned large cargo pockets (for gloves, hat etc) and easily accessible hand warmer pockets. Features such as waist or hem drawcord, close fitting hood, adjustable cuffs (for good ventilation as well as insulation) high collar with wind protective neck closure all help prevent heat loss and keep out wind.

Cut and style is also important to a garments function. A close fitting yet unrestrictive jacket will maintain a layer of insulation underneath whereas a loose fitting jacket loses insulation during movement.

Insulated Jackets

Duvet and synthetic insulated jackets

In very cold conditions, down filled jackets provide the best insulation available combined with low weight and bulk when packed. To maintain insulation in wet climates they need the protection of either a separate shell jacket or a breathable waterproof outer material to prevent the down filling becoming damp, an expensive combination which unless used regularly in extreme winter conditions is not very cost effective.

Although less expensive, synthetic filled jackets, as with down, lack versatility when used in a changeable climate, giving rise to overheating unless used in very cold conditions. The added problem of bulk and weight when packed needs to be considered unless conditions make it necessary to wear the jacket all the time, which is when these jackets come into their own. The use of thinner lighter fillings which despite their low density, provide very good insulation, are being used more by manufacturers now, and fillings currently available are those known under the trade names of Hollofil, Quallofil, Isodry, Thinsulate and Libond.

Ventile

While cotton is not recommended for inner garments in cold damp climates it can be effective when used for outer garments. Fine tightly woven cotton (ventile) is ideal for an outer jacket, combining warmth, comfort and wind resistance with durability. Ventile breathes by allowing moisture vapour to pass through the fibres while remaining windproof. When wet, cotton threads swell or expand making it difficult for rain to pass through. In heavy or continual rain, a shell garment is necessary thus making a heavy combination which can also be bulky when packed! This plus lengthy drying time makes them less popular than synthetic jackets, but if weight is no problem and conditions warrant the jacket being worn most of the time then a ventile jacket is a warm comfortable alternative to synthetics in winter. Extremely good in cold windy conditions but difficult to obtain.

Legwear

Any form of legwear for hill use or mountain environments should allow unrestricted leg movement, be as light and comfortable as possible, windproof and quick drying.

Breeches are excellent year round legwear, made from mixed stretch fabrics they combine freedom of movement with warmth and comfort and allow ventilation to lower legs. Modern stretch fabrics mean designs can be stylish yet still practical. Extra material on knees and seat give greater wearability while other features include large front and rear pockets (some zipped) and adjustable velcro fastened hems.

A range of legwear (shorts, breeches and full length trousers) made from closely woven polycotton are available for mainly summer use, being light, windproof and quick drying. Suitable for general walking but for more serious use, harder wearing mixed fabrics are recommended. Full length polycotton trousers with the addition of soft brushed polyester linings provide good insulation in winter. Features should be the same as those of the harder wearing breeches already mentioned.

Extremities

Feet

It is essential that feet stay well cushioned, warm and dry. Wool is comfortable and warm, retaining warmth when wet. A percentage of synthetic fibres are necessary for added strength and durability but wool content should not be less than 70%. Socks combining ribbed leg with loop stitch pile foot provide cushioning and insulation. If two pairs are worn, loop stitch are better as inner socks with plain or ribbed socks over the top. Size is also important as large or loose fitting socks rub and crease causing blisters and general discomfort. If two pairs are worn, outer socks can crease the inner pair if the outer pair are too small. Available in short or long leg lengths, the latter being preferable when worn with breeches.

Head

Warm headgear is essential in high or exposed places in winter. Headwear performs a dual purpose providing protection from the effects of severe weather and in conserving body warmth both by day and at night. A high percentage of heat is lost through the head and shoulders. Balaclava designs offer full head, neck and face protection and are available in fleece, polypropylene, pile and wool. Synthetics have the advantage over natural fibres, drying rapidly when wet, being extremely comfortable to wear particularly if worn to sleep in on cold nights, and very light.

Hats come in a variety of designs and styles with a whole range of fleece hats available to choose from. Choice should be governed primarily by warmth, comfort, drying time and wind protection particularly the ears. All headgear should fit comfortably under the hood of a waterproof jacket. Finally, in winter it pays to carry a spare dry hat or balaclava for use at night.

Hands

Although hands may not always feel cold during activity they do affect overall body temperature considerably if exposed in cold weather. This is one part of the body which due to the necessity of frequent use can be difficult to insulate in severe winter climates. A versatile method of insulation is necessary to cope with the variety of conditions and situations encountered.

In freezing temperatures, thin silk or polypropylene gloves on their own are inadequate for winter mountain environments yet when worn as part of a combination are essential in many situations. Worn under thermal mitts, they prevent fingers becoming exposed when mitts are taken off in order to operate camera, compass, zips, buckles, stoves etc and when rock scrambling, setting up camp and so on. Mitts, although restrictive, are more effective insulators, utilizing heat generated by the palm keeping fingers warm.

Pile, fleece and woollen mitts are very popular but need the protection of a windproof pertex or microfibre face fabric or more essentially a Gore-Tex overmitt, many of which are available with detachable pile thermal inner mitts.

Keeping dry: Shell clothing

Shell clothing
Clothing that provides insulation traps warm air in its layers and fibres. This is reduced or lost when exposed to outside elements in cold and wet conditions. To prevent this, a layer of shell clothing impervious to wind and rain is needed. This consists of a jacket, overtrousers, overmitts and gaiters.

Materials
Nylon is the most practical fabric for shell garments because it is light, low in bulk and resists moisture absorption. To make nylon waterproof (and hence windproof) it has to be either coated or allied to a waterpoof membrane. The difference between various methods is the degree to which they reduce condensation inside the garment. The most effective methods cost more but are allied to quality garments offering a higher level of comfort and performance.

Coatings

Non breathable
Polyurethane (P.U.) is the most basic, hence cheapest and lightest form of waterproof coating. Although effective initially, it is less durable than other coatings and condensation is a constant problem. Neoprene (a synthetic rubber) although heavier is more effective and durable and in terms of cost is good value for money. As with all types of waterproof clothing, taped seams are a must. Neoprene also suffers from heavy condensation.

Breathable
Hydrophylic coatings provide a cost effective alternative between low cost non
breathable coatings and expensive breathable laminates. Combining light weight

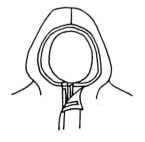

**A jacket hood whether fixed or detach-
ble should be large enough to fit over
warm headwear in winter, yet fit well
enough to keep out driving rain and
snow. An adjustable valence inside the
front of the hood enables closure around
the face without impairing vision when
the hood is closed up.**

with a degree of breathability, hydrophylic coatings work on the principle of moisture vapour transmission (M.V.T.). Condensation is reduced by being pushed along the molecular structure of the coating to the outside of the garment by the difference in humidity between the inside and outside of the garment. Appearance is similar to polyurethane coatings.

Microporous
Microscopic pores in the polyurethane coating allow water vapour to pass through while preventing water droplets getting in. They work on the same principle as hydrophylics. Thickness of coatings vary. The thinner coatings although more breathable are less durable.

Membranes

These are thin films of waterproof material either separate from or laminated to the nylon outer material. Some are protected by a lining on the inside of the garment.

Microporous
Better known under the trade name of Gore-Tex, this has become one of the most successful and effective methods of producing a breathable waterproof garment. The microporous membrane (P.T.F.E.) works in a similar way to the microporous coatings but with a higher level of efficiency. It is available in two or three layer laminates.

Hydrophylic

A solid membrane which works on the same principle as hydrophylic coatings but with an increased rate of moisture vapour transmission. Known under the trade name Sympatex, it offers an alternative to microporous membranes (Gore-Tex) with a distinct advantage. Being a solid membrane as opposed to a microporous one, it is claimed to be more durable, having no pores to get clogged. Its efficiency at reducing condensation for a longer period prior to being washed is worth considering. However, long term durability of the performance of the molecular structure has yet to be proven.

Condensation and breathability

All waterproof nylon garments are prone to condensation buildup inside the garment. The extent to which this occurs depends on the method used to make the garment waterproof, the level of humidity in the atmosphere and the extent of physical exertion. Sustained activity produces greater condensation problems which can be excessive in garments with non breathable coatings.

This problem has been greatly reduced by the development of breathable coatings and membranes. The rate at which condensation is dispersed depends on the ability of the coating or membrane to transmit moisture to the outside of the garment during physical activity. The term 'breathable' refers to the ability of the material to allow moisture vapour to pass through the fabric.

Drop liners

These are free hanging waterproof membranes (at present microporous Gore-Tex) laminated to a thin knitted fabric inserted between the garments inner and outer material, giving improved breathability and a softer feel to the garment.

Waterproof Jackets

Ability to keep you dry is far more important than appearance and style. Worn at times in severe conditions, material needs to be strong and well constructed. Driving rain can find its way into the jacket through seams unless fully taped. Strong material will resist abrasion and wear from a heavy rucksack. An integral or detachable hood is an essential part of any waterproof jacket and should be large enough to fit over a woollen hat or balaclava. A wired visor deflects rain, snow and wind and improves vision. Drawcords around the hood and waist help preserve body temperature by reducing heat loss as do adjustable velcro cuff closures. Drawcords with sliding friction cord grips or spring toggles allow easy adjustment in cold weather.

Varying climatic conditions require continual adjustment to allow good ventilation. Full length double ended zips allow regulation of ventilation as well as permitting extra leg movement when unzipped from the bottom. Fully zipped jackets are easier to put on and off and enable quick closure during sudden showers. Over the head smock designs, although more comfortable, do not have these advantages.

Zips should be heavy duty plastic and covered by velcro or press stud storm flaps.

Pockets

Most jackets have at least two large cargo pockets, designed to keep water entry to a minimum, having protective flaps or closures over external entries. Positioning is important so that items needed frequently can be reached without being restricted by the rucksack hipbelt.

Internal chest pocket should be large enough to hold a map, giving easy access located under the front protective flap, eliminating the need to unzip the jacket when access is required.

Size

A waterproof shell garment should be large enough to fit over several layers of clothing (including a jacket) in winter without being restrictive, and long enough to cover the waist while stretching or bending.

Appearance and style

To find a jacket that fits your requirements, some compromise is necessary when comparing various features on different garments and when considering cost. Consider priorities and make sure that any compromise made is not at the expense of quality and performance. Your life may one day depend on the quality of the garment.

Colour is a personal choice and a controversial point! Environmental colours that blend with the landscape are aesthetically more pleasing than bright fluorescent colours which do have a safety aspect and may be advisable for the novice, but with more experience this aspect becomes less of a consideration. Avoiding extremes does not mean that choice is limited to dull depressing colours. Many recent styles incorporate bright colours in the design, but in a way that co-ordinates colours tastefully, enhancing style and appearance while remaining environmentally acceptable and fashionable without compromising on quality and performance.

Gaiters

Made from cotton duck, proofed nylon or Gore-Tex, gaiters protect lower legs from wet grass, snow, peat and sharp undergrowth. They also prevent the intrusion of snow, mud and small stones into boots. Useful all year round, and in some situations provide an alternative to overtrousers.

Design features include full length zip, drawcord top, elasticated ankle and hem. Fitted with hooks which clip over boot laces at the front and a cord under the instep holds the gaiters over the boot. Some designs completely enclose the boot, fitting into a moulded groove incorporated into certain makes of boots.

Overmitts

Cold winds and shed rain from jacket sleeves both remove insulation from unprotected woollen gloves or mitts. Proofed nylon or Gore-Tex overmitts keep hands and gloves dry and warm in severe conditions.

Elasticated cuffs and wrists prevent heat loss and stop moisture getting in.

Overtrousers

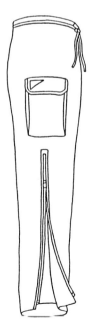

An item needed throughout the year. Construction and materials are similar to shell jackets. A generous cut is important to allow freedom of movement when worn over other legwear. To facilitate being put on and taken off frequently without too much effort, a zipped gusset is essential, the longer the better, avoiding having to remove boots each time!

Additional features include waist drawcord, outside pocket and abrasion resistant material on the lower inside leg.

Some walkers prefer to wear gaiters in wet weather, putting up with upper legs becoming damp rather than having the condensation problem of non-breathable waterproof overtrousers. However, in extreme conditions it is far better to be wet and warm than damp and exposed. This is where overtrousers made from breathable fabrics begin to justify their cost.

Size

Leg length is important. Overtrousers sag when wet and if leg length is too long, the material will wear rapidly at the hem from being dragged along the ground and boots rubbing together when walking. Some makes have the option to shorten the leg length, providing that the gusset zip ends a couple of inches above the hem. A waist that is too tight can restrict circulation and cause discomfort.

Boots

Despite the introduction of lightweight synthetic boots, traditional leather walking boots remain the most practical for year round use. Although at one time quite heavy, new techniques in the manufacturing process has made possible a wide variety of mid-weight general hillwalking boots suitable for year-round use.

Uppers

Constructed ideally from a single piece leather and should include a full leather bellows tongue. The less seams and stitching the better. Uppers will be stronger and less likely to come apart. Leather breathes allowing feet to stay reasonably dry and comfortable. Leather has natural water resistant qualities and allows waterproofing agents to soak in, increasing water resistance and aiding wearing in when new, making the leather more supple.

Ankle support is necessary when carrying heavy loads over rough ground. Padded ankle cuffs prevent rubbing and help stop small stones getting in. Leather should be cut and shaped around the ankle to provide maximum support and comfort. D rings and hooks allow boots to be tightened correctly to the shape of the feet and provide a quick and easy method of lacing.

Linings

Many boots now include a lining which absorbs moisture and cushions the foot, helping to keep feet dry and comfortable. The lining is quick drying and hard wearing adding to the overall comfort and durability of the boot.

Soles

Flexibility is important and soles need to be flexible with directional foot support and cushioning on rough ground. The amount of support and flexibility is determined by the makeup of the midsole. On walking boots, this consists of a moulded nylon flexible stiffener.

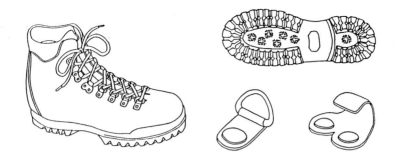

Left: **Year-round midweight leather walking boot, incorporating quality leather upper with minimal stitching, cut and shaped ankle to provide support and integral bellows tongue.** *Top right:* **Vibram Montagna (traditional) sole.** *Bottom right:* **Nickle-plated brass hooks and "D" rings provide quick and easy lacing.**

Thickness tapers to give the right amount of flex and support to various parts of the foot. The amount of thickness and flex varies depending on boot size and intended purpose.

Moulded nylon midsoles combine longitudinal flex with firm lateral support, preventing the boot twisting on uneven ground. Boots intended mainly for climbing or winter use with crampons need a more rigid sole.

Many boots now include a removable footbed contoured to provide heel and arch support for improved comfort. This light-weight hardwearing material helps wick away perspiration and drys out quickly. They can also be replaced easily when worn down.

Sole patterns
Several types of sole pattern are suitable for providing good traction on the variety of terrain encountered in the fells throughout the year. Most well-known are the traditional Vibram montagna soles (illustrated). Skywalk produce a range of sole patterns most of which are highly suitable for general hillwalking situations and conditions.

Soles should provide good grip on most terrains, be hard-wearing and designed to reduce clogging. The Skywalk traction soles incorporate a cleated rounded heel designed to increase traction on downhill slopes and reduce shock when walking on flat surfaces by allowing gradual transition onto the sole without the jarring that occurs with the traditional right-angled heel. Modern methods of manufacture allow soles to be bonded to uppers with only a minimum amount of stitching on some designs to give additional strength for more rugged use. Both Vibram and Skywalk soles can be replaced when necessary. An additional feature of the Skywalk traction sole and featured increasingly on other makes too, is the moulded groove around the sole which accommodates gaiters designed to completely enclose the uppers. Avoid cheap imitations of the better makes of sole patterns. Made from a different compound, they are not so hardwearing and less effective at providing grip on wet rock and steep slopes as well as less overall foot support generally.

Fitting

It is important to find a pair of boots that fit properly. A lot of misery is caused by ill fitting boots. Even identical pairs of boots feel different when worn. Boots differ slightly in size according to make, and always need to be tried on to determine fit. To get some idea of how they will perform, walk round in them while in the shop. Pressure or rubbing to any part of the foot will be amplified the longer they are worn and will give rise to serious problems later. Try several pairs and even a different size for comparison. This will help you select a pair you are happy with. The idea that boots should be one size larger than normal shoe size no longer applies so it pays to be selective. There are also different width fittings. Feet should not feel cramped.

Even if only slightly cramped then the boots are too small. If toes feel cramped, this will cause problems when walking downhill and feet get pushed forward.

How many pairs of socks will be worn? Modern boot technology does away with the need for more than one good pair of socks to be worn unless used mainly in extreme winter conditions. Whatever your preference, wear the appropriate socks when trying boots on. Remember too that feet swell and make allowances accordingly. If socks become compressed insulation will be lost in addition to being uncomfortable.

Alternatively, if boots feel loose, do not try to compensate by tightening laces or with extra socks. Once leather becomes supple, no amount of tightening will compensate if boots are too large. All boots have a slight amount of slip at the heel when new until the initial stiffness has gone. Your heel should only rise a fraction in the boot, any more than this then the boots are too big.

2 Equipment

Backpacks

Worn for the duration of any walk, correct fit and comfort are essential. An ill-fitting rucksack will cause pain, discomfort and fatigue after wearing it for some time so it is important to select one to suit your size and purpose.

This has been made easier by the development of adjustable back systems. Increased comfort and stability are a result of the attention given to design to incorporate load carrying principles so that heavy loads can be carried for long distances over difficult terrain comfortably. Present designs incorporate lightweight integral frames, adjustable contoured back systems, shaped shoulder harness and hip belts.

Capacity

First consideration is carrying capacity. This varies from small day sacks to large expedition sacks of between eighty to one hundred litres. Capacity will depend on the nature and extent of trips and equipment needed. As a guide, equipment necessary for an average two week backpacking trip should fit comfortably into a seventy five litre sack or less if you only take the absolute essentials. A sack with a larger capacity than necessary will encourage over-compensation with equipment to justify the extra space. Whatever time of year you go, you will never have all items in the pack.

In winter, most of your clothing will be worn, in summer less clothing and lighter gear is taken anyway, so work out beforehand what will be carried in the pack at any given time of year and choose the capacity accordingly.

Size

Different from capacity, some sacks have the same capacity but differ in back length, size of hip belt and shoulder harness width. Well designed larger capacity sacks have adjustable back systems, hip belts and shoulder harness. However, some may not adjust enough to suit your height and size if you are a small build and may necessitate selecting a smaller capacity sack.

If the shoulder straps are too far apart they will slip off in use.

Try several makes and sizes until one fits properly, feels comfortable without being either too loose or restrictive when adjusted.

Well-designed backpacking rucksacks allow even distribution of weight, easy access to items needed frequently on route and prevent food and clothing becoming contaminated by stove fuel by having several well-positioned compartments and pockets.

Fitting

To determine the fit, try it on in the shop, making all necessary adjustments both with and without a jacket on. One of the main features of larger sacks is the padded hip belt. This is where most of the weight is carried so it is important that it fits properly and feels comfortable when adjusted. The padded hip belt should rest on the upper part of the hips without causing any pressure around the base of the spine. The back length should then be adjusted so that the sack is as high as possible. On some sacks, this adjustment can be made with the sack on. The shoulder harness should follow the contours of the shoulders without being too tight.

There should be little or no weight transmitted through the shoulder harness. Properly adjusted, the shoulder harness will hold the sack in place against your back aiding stability, the hip belt taking the weight. Fine adjustment can be made to the shoulder harness if the sack is fitted with top tensioning straps, raising the harness above the top of the shoulders slightly and pulling the pack closer to your back improving centre of gravity. Once adjusted, the top of the sack should be about the same height as your head. Some sacks have an alloy internal frame, the strips being malleable to allow the sack to be shaped to suit the curvature of the spine. Ventilation around the small of the back is important and a good sack will be designed to allow this.

Design

Main differences between various makes concerns methods of adjustable back and carrying systems. Packs are similar in design, having a main compartment which on many sacks is divided into an upper and lower section with either a fixed or removable divider. The lower compartment is accessible through a double ended zipped opening around the front of the sack and which is protected by a storm flap. Useful for storing waterproof clothing or larger items needed quickly without having to undo the main sack to get at them. Two external side pockets either fixed or detachable allow stove fuel to be carried separately away from clothing and food and allow it to be readily available along with other small items that may be needed on route. Large lid pockets are useful for maps, first aid kit, emergency rations, hat and gloves etc. A drawcorded extension cover at the top of the main compartment provides protection against rain and snow and extends capacity. Quick release plastic buckles are standard fittings on most sacks, making access easier in cold weather while wearing gloves. Padded back panels and lumbar pad add to overall comfort and aid ventilation.

Materials

All specialised sacks are now made from nylon materials. Nylon has the advantage of being light, quick drying, resistant to rot and low water absorbancy. Produced in various thicknesses, some sacks have harder wearing nylon bases where extra durability is needed. More expensive sacks are made entirely of thicker grade material and carry lifetime guarantees against wear and tear. Some have a softer nylon material used on pack panels and the underside of shoulder harness straps. Polyurethane (P.U.) coating inside the sack gives a degree of water repellancy but does not make them waterproof.

Manufacturers recommend and sometimes supply polythene liners for inside the sack to provide proper protection against the elements which invariably find their way into the best made sacks.

The pack should be adjusted so that the centre of gravity is high and close to the back, giving increased stability and enabling heavy loads to be carried for long distances over difficult terrain with relative comfort. Weight is transmitted through the padded hipbelt while the shoulder harness holds the pack in place.

Packing

However well designed for load carrying, to be effective, a rucksack needs to be correctly packed. Weight should be properly distributed throughout the pack, the heavier items nearer the top and lighter items lower down.

This helps to keep the centre of gravity high and close to the back, aiding stability. For optimum comfort when carrying a full pack, overall weight should not exceed one third of your own bodyweight.

Sleeping Bags

Design

Close fitting tapered bags that enclose the body and head conserve the most heat and provide the best insulation.

Several variations of these designs exist incorporating integral hoods which when closed around the face provide maximum insulation. The closer the fit the better the insulation as well as being light and less bulky when packed. Bags incorporating a boxed foot allow insulation around feet, preventing compression in this area and avoid feeling restricted. A draught collar around the neck of the bag helps prevent heat loss from inside the bag, particularly when sitting up with arms outside the bag. Full length zips are an advantage in warmer weather. The zip should be insulated down its length with a draught collar inside to prevent heat loss through the zip closure. Some designs feature an elasticated body hugging construction, improving loft, hence insulation by reducing dead air space.

Fluting

Vertical fluting around the chest prevents loss of insulation caused by the thinning out of filling in this area which occurs on bags with lateral fluting due to body movement inside the bag. Radial box and double box constructions are found on some expedition bags made in Germany.

Differential cut

This is the difference between the size and cut of the inner and outer material. The inner is cut smaller to allow the filling full loft capability, preventing it being compressed between the two layers of material thus reducing insulation.

Internal construction

The ability of filling to provide maximum insulation depends on extent of loft and the method used to hold it in position. This is

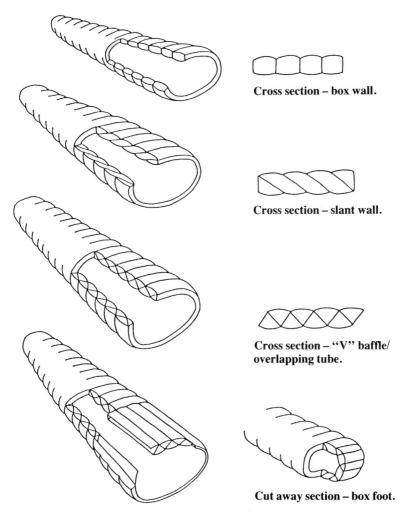

Cross section – box wall.

Cross section – slant wall.

Cross section – "V" baffle/
overlapping tube.

Cut away section – box foot.

Sleeping bags. The cross and cut away sections shows the internal construction method.

achieved by a series of internal walls or baffles sewn between the inner and outer material. Positioning of these internal walls determines the amount of filling used and its distribution. In the case of down and blown synthetic fillings, internal walls ensure correct distribution of filling throughout the bag preventing it from shifting in use, and maintains density of filling in specific areas providing maximum insulation at all times.

Several methods of wall construction include: box wall, slant wall, and overlapping tube constructions. The method used depends on the type of bag and its recommended use.

The simplest method is box wall construction, used mainly on less expensive two season bags. Slant wall construction provides a more even distribution of filling, giving good insulation and preventing cold spots caused by thinning out of filling which can happen with box wall construction. The most effective method is the overlapping tube design used mainly on expedition bags containing down filling, whereas the overlapping shingle method is the most effective form of synthetic construction. These methods allow more filling to be used and consequently is heavier, bulkier and more expensive. Most bags contain side wall baffles to maintain an equal amount of filling on the top and underside of the bag.

Fillings

A sleeping bag should maintain a layer of warm air around the body, providing insulation by trapping body heat and retaining it in the filling. The degree of warmth provided depends on type of filling and amount of loft. Fillings are either down or synthetic. A pile or fleece liner can be used in winter for added warmth, giving the bag an extra seasonal rating.

Down

Down is by far the best insulator available. Bags classed as down filled consist of soft underfeathers of goose or duck combined with a small percentage of ordinary feathers to give loft. While goose down is considered to be the better filling, duck is the most widely used down filling due to its availability and price. Labels show the percentage of down used. The higher the percentage, the warmer, lighter and more compressible the bag will be. Classifications range from: pure down, down/feather to feather/down.

It is down which provides insulation while ordinary feathers give added loft. Feather/down classifications have only a small amount of down and are not recommended for serious backpacking use.

Synthetic

Most synthetic fillings are produced from a polyester fibre and are more commonly known under the trade names Hollofil, Quallofil, Superloft and Microsoft.

Synthetic fillings can be produced in either batt form or by means of the blown filled method. Blown synthetic fillings provide better insulation than fillings produced in batt form. This is because bags using the blown method can be constructed and filled in the same way as down filled bags, making the most of internal space to maximise insulation without too much weight and bulk whereas fillings produced in batt form have to be stitched through to hold the wadding in place, and unless a double layer of wadding is used and overlapped, insulation is lost around the stitching. To be effective a bag would have the inherent problem of weight and bulk making it unsuitable for backpacking.

Down or synthetic?
Both fillings have advantages and disadvantages. Down, on the plus side, is an excellent insulator providing it remains dry. It is light, can be compressed very small and has long term loft capabilities.

Disadvantages include poor insulation when wet or damp, difficult to wash and is expensive. Synthetic fillings are less expensive than down, maintain insulation when wet, easy to wash and warm. Main problems are bulk, weight and relatively short term loft capability when compared with down. Synthetic fillings are ideal for situations where the bag is subject to damp or wet conditions.

Ratings
The type of bag you need will depend on when and where you will use it. Sleeping bags are classified according to the number of seasons they effectively maintain their recommended insulation value or temperature rating. Five season bags can be used in the coldest climates. Four season bags are suitable for use year-round including high level winter use in this country. Three season bags can also be used all year round depending on where you use them. The addition of a fibre pile lining can extend the capability of a three season bag to that of a four season rating. Two season bags are for summer use only but can be extended with the use of a lining.

Some manufacturers give a temperature rating along with a seasonal rating but it should be remembered that this is an approximate guide which applies when the bag is new and varies from one manufacturer to another.

Too warm or too cold?
The ideal solution to our varying climate is to have a bag for each season. Because this is not always financially possible, an all rounder has to be sought. This involves a certain amount of compromise one way or another. Better to compromise by being too warm at times rather than too cold in winter. Many of the bags for use in colder climates have full length zips (left or right) and can be opened out and used like a duvet cover during summer months.

Insulation mats
However good the sleeping bag may be, insulation is reduced when compressed by bodyweight. The use of an insulation mat provides protection from cold ground and compensates insulation

lost by compression of the bag filling. Insulation mats provide extra cushioning and protect both the bag and tent groundsheet from sharp objects when placed under groundsheet material. Closed cell foam mats have no water absorbancy, do not lose insulation under compression and are very light. Open cell foam absorbs water and is not recommended unless inside a waterproof nylon shell and even then can be quite bulky. Mats are available in different widths, lengths and thicknesses, and should be light, non absorbant, tear resistant and be able to recover quickly from compression.

Lightweight Tents

Function
A major item of equipment, this lightweight portable shelter has to provide protection against the worst type of weather with ability to withstand heavy rain, strong winds and drifting snow in exposed places, so quality and suitability are important. Specialist lightweight tents are expensive so care and consideration should be given to selecting a tent to suit your needs. Designs each have their own advantages depending on where they are used.

Some tents are recommended only for low level use while others are designed for year round high level use. Where and when will it be used? Cost permitting, it is better to choose a tent with an all purpose year round capability. Even if you restrict yourself to low level camping initially, you will eventually want to extend your experience to high level camping in winter. This is a natural progression and although expensive initially, will be cost effective in the long term.

Size
Will a one or two person tent suit your needs? This classification is only an approximate guide to the size of a tent. Consider internal space. Headroom and storage space are important in bad weather. One person tents can be cramped with little or no room for movement or equipment.

In winter, more time is spent inside the tent and two person tents provide more room for equipment and cooking in bad weather with only a slight increase in weight and packed size. Always check and compare dimensions before buying and make sure the inner is long enough.

Materials
The use of nylon has given rise to a whole range of backpacking tents and is now used for all lightweight tent designs. Silicon

treated nylon or polycotton breathable inners prevent condensation from outer material soaking through. Cotton is also used for tent inners. As well as being light, nylon tents pack small, dry quickly and do not rot. The main problem is condensation buildup inside the polyurethane coated flysheets. Outer tent material varies in thickness according to the purpose intended. Some tents have rip-stop nylon flysheets which are lighter with equivalent strength. Groundsheet material should be an integral part of the inner tent, forming the first few inches of the inner tent walls. Groundsheet proofings vary. To keep weight to a minimum, many tents have polyurethane coated groundsheets. Recently, an increasing number of manufacturers are using slightly heavier but more durable neoprene coatings while some use a P.V.C. coating.

The quality of materials and construction is just as important to the overall strength and stability of a tent as the design itself. Good stitching along seams and around stress points is important. Any weakness or bad workmanship in these areas will soon give rise to problems when exposed to rough weather. Straight evenly spaced stitching should run the entire length of seams. Pegging points and areas around poles should be reinforced and bar tacked. Seams should be folded and sewn flat (lap felled method). Some tents now have taped seams. Groundsheet seams should be minimal if any and ideally avoid running across an area of the groundsheet that is subject to constant pressure.

Design
Having some idea of the category and size, comparisons can be made between various designs within that category. Factors which influence lightweight tent design are: maximum internal space, minimum weight, stability, weather protection, ease of pitching, strength of materials and packed size. Due to the variety of tent designs it is difficult to know which would be the most suitable for your purpose. Tent design depends on which factors have been considered more advantageous for the intended purpose. Consider which of these factors is most important to your requirements. The design you need will then be predetermined by these prior considerations.

A tent must be easy to put up as pitching in strong winds or in the dark is sometimes necessary. A design which allows the fly-sheet to be pitched first is an advantage when raining.

Tent assembly
Methods of tent assembly vary but fall into one of two categories when it comes to pitching double skin tents: either flysheet or inner first. Flysheet first designs enable the inner to remain dry

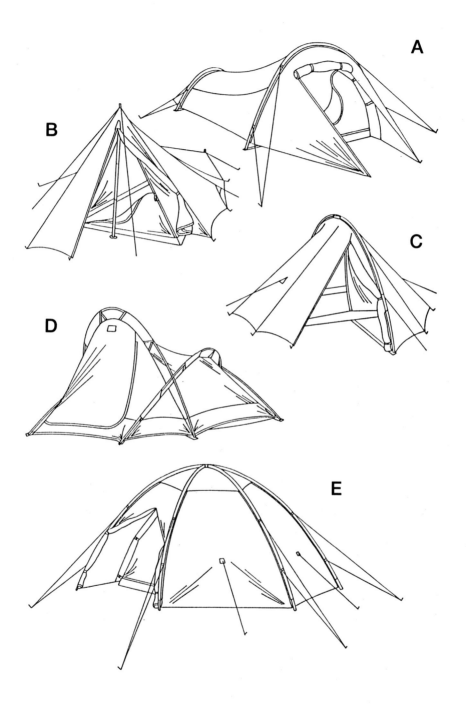

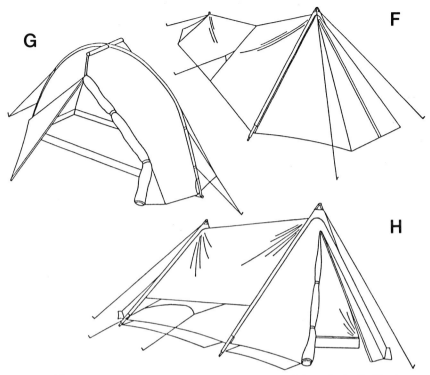

Tents. A. Twin hoop tunnel; B. Sloping ridge (upright poles); C. Single hoop (transverse); D. Free standing geodesic; E. 3-pole dome; F. Sloping ridge ("A" pole); G. Single hoop (lateral); H. Parallel ridge mountain tent (twin "A" poles).

when pitching and packing in bad weather. Although easy to pitch, inners are suspended from the flysheet and tend to flap in windy conditions. The problem is lessened considerably with tents that pitch inner first and include many of the flexi pole designs. Poles fit through sleeves sewn to the inner, holding the material taut. The flysheet then fits tightly over the poles producing a stable structure.

Double and single skin tents
The majority of lightweight tents are double skin designs. Although heavier, double skin designs can be warmer and more versatile than single skin tents. The space between the inner and outer (usually about ten centimetres) provides some insulation, adding to the overall comfort, warmth and protection offered. On occasions the outer can be used separately if the design allows. To help retain warmth, the flysheet should completely enclose the

inner on all sides. Nearly all designs have a large bell end or protective porch at the front which can be used for equipment storage and cooking in bad weather.

The use of Gore-Tex breathable materials has resulted in several new designs of single skin tents with the advantages of less weight to space ratio, small packed size, and a reduction in the condensation problem encountered on double skin tents. Ideal throughout most of the year and where pack weight has to be kept to a minimum but problems can arise in conditions where the humidity level inside the tent is lower than on the outside, giving rise to condensation. To be effective, breathable materials will only work efficiently if humidity is higher inside the material.

Several design concepts are available and include the ridge, sloping ridge, wedge, tunnel, single hoop, dome and geodesic designs. These can be split into two main categories: rigid pole tents which includes 'A' pole and various ridge designs and: flexi pole tents which include the tunnel, single hoop, dome and geodesic designs.

Rigid pole tents

Ridge tents are the most traditional designs and now have the advantages of modern lightweight tent technology incorporated into them, resulting in suitable all purpose year-round tents.

Various designs based on the ridge concept are available and incorporate either twin alloy 'A' poles, front 'A' pole and rear upright, front and rear upright or a front transverse ridge and rear upright pole arrangement.

'A' poles provide good stability in rough weather, allow easy access and are easy to pitch. The angled roof sheds snow easily but limits internal space. Twin 'A' pole arrangements although heavier, are the most suitable high level year-round designs. Sloping ridge and wedge designs are much lighter and reduce the effect of wind when pitched with the lower end windward.

Upright pole supports are less stable than 'A' pole supports and depend on good guying for stability in bad weather, making a good flat pitch essential. Depending on where used, sloping ridge and wedge tents can be used year round and will provide adequate bad weather protection in sheltered areas.

Flexi pole tents

The introduction of lightweight flexible pole materials has given rise to a new generation of lightweight tents. These include the tunnel, single hoop, dome and geodesic designs. An advantage of the flexi pole designs is the greater internal space/weight ratio created by the arch arrangement of the poles. These are similar on all designs, being either fibreglass or flexible alloy.

Designs of tent differ according to the number of poles used, their length and arrangement.

Tunnel designs usually incorporate two or three parallel pole supports, sometimes of equal length, sometimes of differing lengths depending on design. All provide good headroom and internal space. Stability is generally good, these designs provide an alterntive to sloping ridge designs.

Single hoop designs use one long pole support, either transversely or lengthways. These designs offer excellent weight to space ratio as well as good stability in rough weather.

Dome designs make the most use of internal space. The cross-over pole arrangement holds outer tent material taut, reducing wind flap and giving excellent stability. Although heavier, the greater internal space and stability are worth considering for year-round or bad weather use. The design gives good wind and rain shedding ability and the ability to flex in strong winds allows pressure to be absorbed and spread over a greater surface area avoiding concentrated stress on any one point.

Geodesic designs are becoming popular with many backpackers. The lightweight two and three pole models are very stable designs, the self-supporting pole arrangements provide rigidity, reduces wind flap and maximises internal space. These designs overcome many of the problems inherent in other lightweight tent designs. Although generally regarded as three season tents, they can be used year-round in sheltered areas.

Poles and pegs

Pole types depend on tent design. Rigid alloy poles are used on ridge designs, fibreglass or flexible alloy on tunnel, single hoop, dome or geodesic designs. Poles are either separate or shock-corded together, the latter being essential for pole assemblies that have to be fed through nylon sleeves sewn to tent material. Several designs of pegs cater for various ground conditions and types of tent. Inner tents need only straight alloy pegs while stronger pegs are necessary for flysheets and guylines.

Angled steel pegs with crimped edges are suitable for most ground conditions. Heavy duty plastic pegs are ideal for guy lines and main anchorage points where stress occurs.

Although tents are supplied with appropriate sets of pegs, an extended range of pegs will suit all types of ground conditions throughout the year.

Seasonal ratings

By their nature, protection offered by lightweight tents is limited during extreme weather conditions and in exposed places, particularly high up. All lightweight tents should be pitched in sheltered areas wherever possible.

Tents with 3 season ratings can be used year round if used in sheltered low lying areas in winter. A 4 season rating means the tent can be used (sensibly) in less sheltered areas and at higher altitudes. Always avoid pitching on sites prone to strong winds.

Lightweight single burner stoves and equipment

High altitude and cold temperatures effect the performance of certain types of fuel. In sheltered low level areas, any fuel or stove arrangement can be used successfully, but only a few types are suitable for year round all weather hill use.

Select a stove and fuel which will perform effectively in all conditions. Examples include the Coleman Peak 1 petrol stove, Trangia meths stove, and the range of Optimus stoves which include the Trapper storm stove, a sturdy meths burner with an integral pan set and wind shield, the model 96 mini camper paraffin burner, the model 8R Hunter petrol burner and the S.V.E.A. 123R Climber petrol burner which is one of the lightest and simplest stoves to operate. A growing range of multiple fuel burning stoves are available from various manufacturers. These are just a few of the most well known examples of stoves available at present which are tried and tested, hence reliable in all conditions.

Consideration of some important fundamental features will help in selecting the most suitable stove for your purpose. The stoves mentioned all use liquid fuels. These are: petrol, paraffin and methylated spirits.

Petrol and paraffin stoves burn fuel under pressure, mixing vaporised fuel with air to give a high heat output which remains efficient in cold temperatures and high altitude.

Meths stoves are simple, safe and easy to use requiring neither priming or pressurising. To be effective, the burner needs to be well shielded. Both the Trangia stormcooker and Optimus trapper incorporate integral pan supports and windshields that utilize wind to increase performance. Ideal in unsheltered conditions but bulky when packed.

Fuel

All types of fuel have advantages and disadvantages. Consider availability, cost, heat output, performance in bad weather, consumption rate and safety. Petrol stoves require the use of unleaded petrol or Coleman fuel available in most outlets. Priming or preheating is required to vaporise the fuel and can be done by using fuel from the stove. Under pressure, petrol provides a high heat output and is efficient in wind. Disadvantages are its cost and low ignition point, making it quite volatile.

Paraffin stoves require a separate fuel for priming, either meths or pre-heating paste. Paraffin gives a similar performance to petrol and is cheaper.

Meths stoves are the easiest to operate needing no priming, and the safest, not burning under pressure. They can be less effective than petrol or paraffin in wind unless the flame is well shielded. Consumption rate is relatively high, thus more fuel needs to be carried or made available on long trips.

Stove unit

Stoves need to be stable, easy to assemble and simple to operate. A wide base is essential on uneven surfaces and in wind. Consider the effect the weight of a full pan will have on the stove when set up, making sure the combined weight and height will not make the unit unstable. A stove that is easy to assemble and simple to operate is a great advantage in cold and severe conditions.

Tank capacity is important too as burning time, weight and packed size all depend on the size of the tank and amount of fuel carried. Boiling time depends on the fuel used and how well shielded the burner and pan support is. A well shielded burner will greatly increase efficiency, reducing boiling time and save on fuel.

Pan sets

The Trangia and Optimus trapper stoves have purpose designed pansets, ideal for two or three people and comprise several items that when packed nest together neatly. Many smaller individual pan sets are available for solo use. A good example is the Stormy range manufactured by Markill, designed to fit specific stoves. Sets include stainless steel windshields which fit over the burner unit, providing maximum heat to the pan. After use, stoves can be packed inside the cookpans. Another feature of these sets is that the unit can be suspended by a chain while in use.

Other sets are available in various sizes. A basic set should comprise at least one pot of 1.5 pint capacity for boiling, together with a lid and a separate pan for frying. Alternatively, a two pot plus frypan set offers more versatility for solo use. Pans should be made of strong lightweight aluminium. Deep pans are preferable to wide shallow pans which lose heat by spreading it over a wider area, resulting in food cooling more quickly around the edges. Packed size, shape, weight, capacity and durability should be considered. A separate pot grab is better than fixed handles which get hot. Some sets incorporate a small lightweight kettle, designed to nest into the pans when packed.

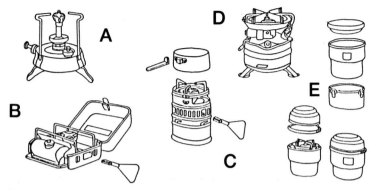

Stoves and equipment. A. Optimus Mini Camper (paraffin); B. Optimus Hiker (petrol); C. Optimus Climber (petrol); D. Coleman Peak I (petrol); E. Markill Stormy Cookset (for Peak I).

Fuel containers

All liquid fuels, particularly petrol, should be carried in metal containers. Optimus and Markill produce a range of aluminium bottles for this purpose. Preventing leakage in transit is very important and tops and caps should be examined closely. Optimus Sigg bottles have leakproof screw tops and are available in different colours to distinguish fuel from drinks. Available in a variety of shapes and sizes, they are strong, light and well sealed and fit easily into rucksack side pockets. Additional screw tops with plastic pipes provide a quick, easy and clean alternative to using a funnel when filling stoves.

Compasses

Why necessary?

Although small and relatively inexpensive compared to other items of equipment, a compass is no less important. In fact, the success of an expedition however small, often depends on it! It may not always be used depending on visibility and how good your map reading skills are, nevertheless, a compass should always be carried.

In good visibility, with the exception of large areas of flat featureless terrain, it takes a secondary role to map reading, helping to confirm direction by identifying features and in setting the map. In poor visibility and on featureless terrain its use when navigating is primary.

Which type of compass?

Several well known manufacturers (examples include Silva, Suunto and Recta) produce a variety of compasses to suit varying needs ranging from simple to highly technical models designed for

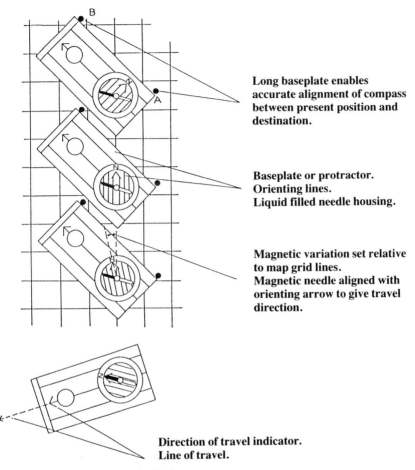

Long baseplate enables accurate alignment of compass between present position and destination.

Baseplate or protractor.
Orienting lines.
Liquid filled needle housing.

Magnetic variation set relative to map grid lines.
Magnetic needle aligned with orienting arrow to give travel direction.

Direction of travel indicator.
Line of travel.

Important features of a field compass.

specialised uses. Choice will largely depend on the degree of accuracy required.

For serious outdoor use, the minimum requirement necessary to cover most navigational problems is a compass designed for use with field maps such as the Ordnance Survey Outdoor Leisure maps (1:25.00) and Landranger (1:50.000) series. This type of compass, known as the field or protractor-compass, includes numbered graduation markings and has a substantial baseplate which acts as the protractor. These features are essential in obtaining accurate bearings to and from the map. The longer the base, the greater the accuracy when direction finding over long distances. A liquid filled needle housing dampens needle swing,

35

aiding the needle to remain steady in use. The housing needs to be sufficiently raised to enable easy rotation when used with gloved hands or cold fingers.

Dial markings should be easy to read and precise. Orienting lines on the underside of the needle housing provide accurate alignment with map grid lines and an orienting arrow marking will also help you to line-up the magnetic needle accurately when following a bearing. All these features are important in assuring accuracy particularly over longer distances or at night.

As with most other items of equipment, field compasses have their limitations! It should be remembered that such compasses are only accurate to within 2°, which over long distances can lead to a considerable error. A sighting compass can provide greater accuracy when fixing and following bearings over longer distances but is largely dependent on good visibility in order to maintain its advantage. For improved accuracy while on the move (a situation where going off-course is most likely to occur) a new type of compass has recently been developed. Produced by Silva, it incorporates a plastic needle rather than a magnetic one. The plastic needle is fixed to a magnet which maintains constant needle direction and virtually eliminates needle swing!

Direction finding is only one aspect of compass use. Calculating distances and locating objectives accurately are also necessary for good navigation. Scales incorporated into the baseplate should include both metric and imperial markings for measuring distances. Romer scales of various sizes enable six figure grid references to be worked out to pin-point positions on maps with corresponding scales.

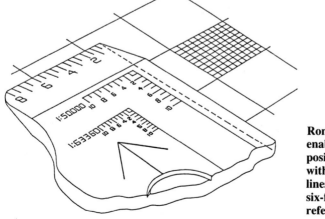

Romer scales enable accurate position-finding within map grid lines using six-figure grid references.

Checking compass accuracy

While the majority of field compasses have a tolerance of 2°, the more expensive models such as the prismatic can achieve accuracy down to ½°. However it is not always necessary to go to such expense to obtain a high degree of accuracy. A simple method of checking the precision of any compass while in the shop will identify the extent of inaccuracy (if any) thus reducing the margin of error within the permitted tolerance.

Line up edge of compass base-plate with grid lines on map. Turn dial until orienting lines and arrow on base of housing are parallel to edge of base-plate and map grid lines. N mark should be directly over marker on dial. If slightly out of alignment, note amount of inaccuracy. This is either due to lines on base of housing being out of line or the needle housing itself being offset in the base plate. Check also the accuracy of orienting arrow on base of housing in relation to orienting lines.

Maps

Maps recommended for use in conjunction with these types of compasses are the Ordnance Survey Outdoor Leisure and Landranger maps, and Harveys walkers maps. These maps contain the detail necessary for accurate navigation using the field compass and include national grid lines which are absolutely essential to a number of compass direction finding techniques.

Winter

Winter accessories

In winter conditions in the hills and mountains, walking on hard packed snow and ice can be dangerous, if not fatal without the use of ice-axe and crampons. In these conditions, these items should be considered absolutely essential and not just optional extras.

Ice axe and crampons

Walking up or across snow slopes can be hazardous and the use of an ice axe is essential for safety. Ice axes come in a number of shapes and sizes, the walkers axe being the type having the longer shaft and an axehead incorporating a standard curved pick with adze. In the event of a fall, the axe can be used for self arrest by a technique involving the use of the pick. The adze is used for cutting steps up hard packed snow slopes. The handle or shaft of a walkers axe being longer than a climbing axe handle enables it to aid balance while traversing snow slopes. When climbing steep slopes, the shaft can be driven into the snow and used as an anchor, or to pull yourself up a slope by firmly fixing the pick into the snow.

Correct shaft length is important and sizes range between 60cm and 80cm lengths at 5cm increments. As a guide to selecting the correct length, the spike should just touch the top of your foot when held downwards by the axehead.

Inward facing teeth along the inside edge of the pick provide grip when dug into hard packed snow. A rubber handle grip, although not fitted to all models, is nevertheless necessary, not only for extra grip but also for insulation. A wrist loop or lanyard attached to the axehead will prevent it rapidly disappearing down a snowslope in the event of it being dropped.

Another essential item of equipment for safe winter mountain walking is a pair of crampons. On hard snow and ice, cleated rubber soles lose their grip. Crampons (spiked metal soles) can be strapped to boots to enable safe walking on this type of terrain.

There are various types of crampons to suit particular requirements. Rigid crampons are suitable only for the more rigid climbing boots and are totally unsuitable for more general mixed terrain walking. Those having an articulated or spring steel flexible adjustment bar are specifically designed for use with walking boots.

Adjustment in length and width is important to allow correct fitting, on more than one pair of boots if necessary. If they fit correctly, they will not fall off when the boots are shaken with the bindings left undone. Methods of attachment vary. Some fit any make of boot while others (mainly step-in bindings) will only fit certain types of boots. Number of points vary too, ranging from 4 point instep crampons (ideal on higher or exposed flat ground where snow has become hard packed and smooth), to 12 point flexible crampons suitable for mixed conditions. 10 and 12 point crampons have two forward facing front points for support when climbing steep snowslopes using the technique known as 'front pointing'.

Winter emergencies
The mountains in winter can offer a far more rewarding experience than at other times of the year. Winter hillwalking is a far more serious endeavour than in summer for many obvious reasons. Not only because the temperature drops dramatically but also because many ordinary basic mountain walking techniques require a much higher degree of skill and ability to perform under much more severe conditions. Navigation becomes critical as snow and ice obscure footpaths and landmarks. Blizzards and heavy mist make the ground indistinguishable from the horizon, a serious situation on or near a ridge or mountain top. Rapidly changing weather conditions or an accident can lead to an enforced night out.

It is essential to be equipped for such an emergency by carrying extra food, clothing and shelter. Spare headwear and gloves are important in case one of these items is accidentally lost. Such items can disappear in seconds if dropped in a wind on top of a mountain, leaving head or hands dangerously exposed.

A bivvy bag is worth its weight in gold and can be a life-saver in an emergency, particularly in winter. It is worth keeping in mind that however good a bivvi-bag may be at keeping out wind and rain, it will not help to insulate your body from the effects of cold temperatures unless used over a sleeping bag.

This guide deals with only one aspect of mountain walking, namely the EQUIPMENT! If you are not familiar or experienced with the mountain and moorland environment, particularly in winter, you should learn the necessary skills BEFORE setting out on your own!

Softwear

Many relevant publications discuss in detail, skills and techniques needed for safe and successful year-round mountain walking. Such publications provide a basic knowledge and understanding about the fundamentals of navigation (map reading, route planning, compass and hillwalking techniques) use of ice axe and crampons etc.

In conclusion

Familiarity breeds contentment! Before setting out, become thoroughly familiar with every aspect of your equipment. This includes performance, handling characteristics and the limitations of each item of equipment under all conditions. A refined, well-developed routine is also essential when setting up camp in bad weather and when packing and getting on the move quickly.

Determine the best method of packing the rucksack to give the most comfortable and stable carry as well as providing easy access to necessary items on route. Become acquainted with basic skills and techniques necessary for year-round fell walking. The fundamentals of navigation including map reading, compass techniques and route planning, along with other skills such as hillwalking skills, campcraft, basic first aid. The use of ice axe and crampons in winter should be familiar to you before setting out on a trip of any length whatever time of year. There is no advantage in having the best equipment available unless you know how to use it!

Care of Clothing and Equipment

Special care and considerations

Quality equipment should be treated as an investment, the return on it being personal safety and success at times when poorer quality equipment would place you in danger, letting you down when you need it most!

This naturally depends on how well you look after your investment, both during and after use. A little care and attention keeps it in prime condition and ensures performance at all times. Before selecting equipment it is useful to know something about the special needs involved in caring for it properly.

Clothing

Regular washing preserves both life and efficiency of garments. Not to be overlooked is the psychological value fresh clean clothes have on morale, especially when worn next to the skin! Care should be taken when washing garments made from synthetic fibres. If subjected to high temperatures during washing and drying, fibres and fibre coatings become damaged, destroying their ability to function properly. This is particularly true of polypropylene/ polyester garments used mainly for first layer clothing with ability to 'wick'. Having a low melt point, low heat settings are necessary when washing and drying, otherwise ability to conduct moisture (wicking) will be lost.

"Breathable" waterproof shell garments
A common mistake made by many who buy expensive breathable shell garments for the first time is to think that, because clothing worn underneath has become quite damp, the garment has failed in some way. While this may be the case in one or two isolated instances, it is not the reason generally. What is worn underneath a "breathable" shell garment will drastically affect its performance. Cotton garments, for example, will absorb moisture from the body and hold it in its fibres. Once wet, moisture cannot pass through and the shell garment cannot transport moisture, only moisture vapour. This then totally negates the effectiveness of breathable systems.

It is important to wear garments that will not absorb moisture vapour and will allow it to pass through the fibres to the breathable shell garment where it can be transported to the outside of the material, thus keeping the inner garments relatively dry.

Boots

Although leather has natural waterproof qualities, natural oils soon wash out when worn in wet weather and the resultant underfoot conditions on the hills. Regular attention helps maintain resistance to water and keeps boots supple. If oils are not replaced regularly and the leather dries out completely, it will crack and soak up water next time out.

Boot manufacturers recommend specific treatments for their products, either in liquid form or one of several wax preparations now available. Designed to penetrate into the leather, they keep it both supple and water repellent. Ordinary polish is not generally recommended because it does not penetrate and soon wears off in use. Some quality leathers however, require minimal preparation initially due to the characteristics of the leather and treatment applied to it during the tanning process. When applying treatment to these boots, follow the manufacturers instructions, using only recommended preparations as some solvent based proofing agents adversely affect the performance of specially treated leathers.

Down sleeping bags

Special care should be taken when handling down bags during washing. When wet, down clumps together becoming heavy. Unless lifted carefully along its length, the weight of the wet down will cause internal walls to collapse. Wash down bags in a bath for ease of handling. After soaking for the recommended time (depending on which cleaning agent is used) allow the water to drain off, then rinse several times until the water runs clear. Gently PRESS out as much excess water as possible and carefully spin dry until all remaining moisture is removed. The bag can then be dried naturally by being placed over a washing line, or tumble dried on a low heat setting. Clumps of down need to be broken up during the drying process to ensure an even distribution of filling.

Alternatively, a reputable professional cleaning agency may be equipped to do the job for you but check first that the process and chemicals used will not destroy or reduce the natural properties of the down. If you do wash the bag yourself, use only recommended down soaps which do not harm or wash away natural oils. These instructions also apply to down filled jackets.

Tent Care

To keep your tent in prime condition, take precautions to protect it from damage when in use. Before pitching, clear the ground of sharp objects that could puncture the groundsheet. An insulation mat placed under groundsheet material provides extra protection. Pitch away from trees and overhanging rocks which shed debris in winds and storms.

Outer tent material, particularly on ridge designs, should be pegged out firmly. Loose material flaps violently in strong winds causing excessive wear and stress leading to failure either of material or the tent structure. Nylon tents go slack after a short time in wet weather and guy lines and pegging points will need re-tightening. After use, dry out tent material if damp and store loosely folded to avoid impairing (cracking) waterproof coating along crease lines.

Unless taped, seal seams before use with the recommended sealant. This may need doing periodically.

OVER & UNDER

MIDDLE LANE, KETTLEWELL, SKIPTON
NORTH YORKSHIRE, BD23 5QX

Proprietor: G. N. Mollard

☎ Kettlewell **0756 760871**

★ Outdoor clothing. ★ Specialist equipment for climbing, caving and backpacking. ★ Lamp and caving equipment hire. ★ Advice on walks, caving and climbing from professionals. ★ Organised instruction in caving and climbing by Nationally Qualified staff. ★ S.R.T. courses. ★ Cave leadership training and assessments. ★ Management Development courses. ★ Fine gifts, Prints, Photographs and Collectors Toy Soldiers. ★ Mail Order. ★ VISA and ACCESS.